FIREBIRD

a poetic journey
of awakening
the inner fire

Alexander Schieffer

with Cosmograms by Marko Pogačnik
UNESCO Artist for Peace, 2016

Home for Humanity Press

Published in 2017 by HOME FOR HUMANITY PRESS
"Home for Humanity" – Domaine de Rachet
Hotonnes en Haut Valromey
01260 France

*All proceeds from our publications support the transformative
education and programs conducted at Home for Humanity.*

Cover Illustrations by Marko Pogačnik
Design and Layout by Moritz Besel

ISBN: 978-2-9560517-0-1

to the firebird

in each one of us

content

foreword

by ashok gangadean, phd

((poetics)): the significance of ((firebird: a poetic journey of awakening the inner fire))

alexander schieffer is a ((poet-philosopher))* in the spirit of heidegger's innovative insight that the essence of philosophy is poetically expressed: to have a ((poetic)) encounter with ((the word)).

in this ((poetic)) sense, the journey of philosophy, the art of wisdom, is a poetic encounter with the ((primal word)), the ((infinite logos)) ((the fire of awareness)).

alexander's ((poetic journey)) is a classic journey from everyday words to the primal logos- ((a poetic journey of awakening the inner life)).

this is our evolutionary ((journey)) from /word/* to ((word)).

his ((four movements)):

((evocation: igniting the flame))

((initiation: approaching the fire))

((involution: stepping into the fire))

((elevation: rising from the ashes))

constitute a powerful ((crossing)) from /word/ to ((word)).

the "reader" is provoked, invoked, seduced, through his ((power words)) into being a ((reader)) ... risen from the (((/ashes/))).

this poetic ((journey)) from /word/ to ((word)), from /reader/ to ((reader)) is our sacred journey into our ((inner fire)).

each ((poem)) is a potent ((meditation)), awakening the ((source words)) that lay dormant in our psyche. his poetic ((journey)) is a journey of ((resurrection)).

alexander is a gifted ((source artist)).

ashok gangadean, phd
margaret gest professor of global philosophy
haverford college, pennsylvania, usa

* When encountered in a ((global light)) the emergent consensus of our great wisdom, enlightenment and scriptural traditions concur that it is highest urgency in our evolutionary maturation for our human family to make the great dimensional crossing from /monologue/ to ((Dialogue)). For decades I have introduced and used"/.../" ("single brackets") to mark when we are lodged in patterns of /monologue/ which sever us from our ((Source Life)), and "((...))" ("double brackets") to make evident when we live and speak from our ((Source Life)).

prelude

the firebird

firebird

the light
you're longing for
is lit !

it's now for you
to feed your flame
and make your life a fire

so hot
it melts the weapons of the world
warms up the hearts of humankind
transforms our hatred into love

leap in !

surrender
to your flame

then, as a bird of fire
spread your wings and soar

for all to feel your might
for all to see the hidden truth of life

igniting the flame

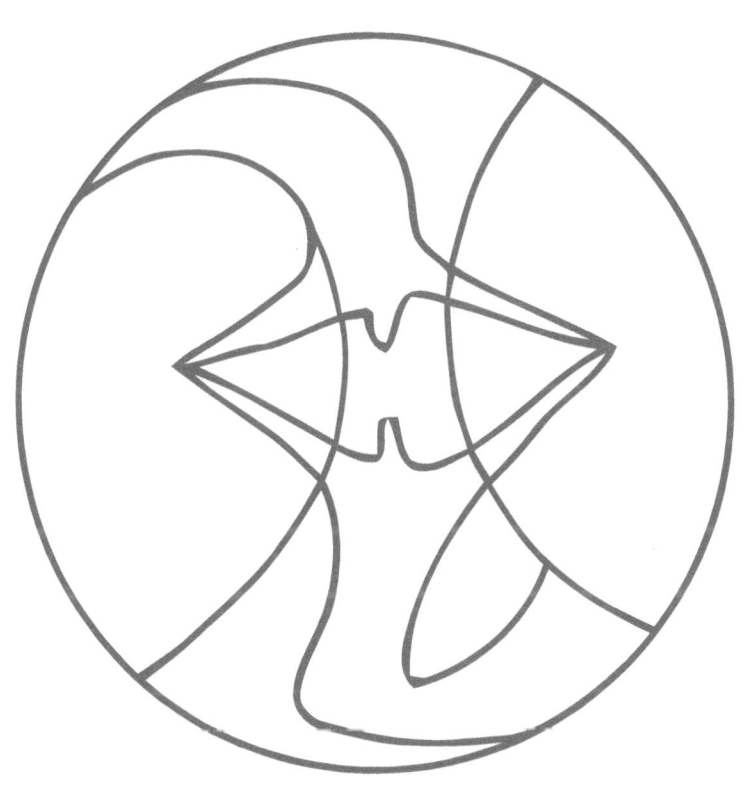

my duty

it's not my duty
to give voice
to the sublime sound
of gently falling summer rain drops
nor to the subtle fragrance
of a newly blooming spring flower bed

let ordinary poets
do that work

my duty is
to give voice
to the desperate yearning
of the god within you
to the song of the heavens
waiting to be birthed in your soul
to the ancient teachings
that await you
once you surrender
to the vast unknown

such verses
are carved out
from the quarries
of atlantis

tell me
my friend
what poetry
is read by your heart ?

unearthing

my saddest poem
is about to be unearthed

for centuries
it lay forgotten
buried in my grounds

its words
too painful
to be spoken

charged with a universe
of guilt and shame
of countless generations

sealed in an iron coffin
with no keys

exploring deeper depths
one recent day
I hit its surface

and in that moment
something in me knew
remembered

since then
I gently burn
the iron layers

and as the lid gets thinner

a tearful whisper
rises from within

my saddest poem
is about to be unearthed

I. evocation

sore hearts

our hearts are sore
more than they ever were
we see the blood of our children everywhere
of our women, old and young,
of our men, emasculated, naked

tell us, oh wise one, where to go
show us a way to peace
that cuts through rolling tanks
and flying bullets
through hatred, torture,
prisons, walls and exile !

and if there were a path
who is still here to walk it ?

wise one, let us grow hearts
much bigger than we ever had
and let us walk that path
one last and final time

walk with us, please, and know
if once again we are deceived
do not replant the seed
of hope in our soil and souls

earth cry

my friend
what has the world
to say about you ?

did you employ the gifts
you once received
from mother earth
to keep her strong ?

where have you been
when she was ripped
of all her riches ?
when she was stripped
stark naked, year by year ?

have you not heard her cry
her torment and her rage ?

do you not know
that every tear she sheds
is just another step
towards her end
and yours ?

wake up and rise
as she gave rise to you
become her faithful lover
in everything you do

why ?

the willingness
to fight
another
for his god
her faith
their race
for land, oil
diamonds
minerals
revenge
you name it

why ?

sheer ignorance
is at its core
the lack
to see
oneself
as source
abundant, full
of endless treasures

of all required
to give birth
to brighter heavens
on this darkened earth

to father-mother
a new human phase
of ever-giving
ever-living
inner-outer space
of ever-glowing
ever-flowing
traceless love and grace

loving when bombs fall

in good times
loving becomes easy !

but loving
when bombs fall
when women are raped
when children of war die of hunger
when your own heart cries nothing but
"revenge !", "kill !" and "no mercy !" ...

... is the greatest art
we are capable of

it's the one road
to heaven
on earth

what's left to say ?

what's left to say
in times like ours ?

perhaps no syllable, no word, no phrase
remains worth uttering

awakening wants stillness
wordlessness

soulsearching graciousness
uncompromising spaciousness

a lotus bud
unfolds at dawn
and in its center
sits the priceless pearl
of newborn knowing

bereft of words

bereft of words and worth
l left my dying world behind
in agony, yet l kept going ...

... knowing

l was growing
life eternal
in my womb

wrapped up for rebirth

and what if
all humanity
went dormant
for a year or two ?

engulfed in dreams
of peaceful futures

eclipsing memories
of self-repeating pasts
of rivalries and wars

...

then, early, one fine day
we all woke up
to higher possibilities

would we not love
to lie together
this one year or two ?

wrapped up for rebirth
arm in arm ?!

return of the goddess

guanyin
shekinah
shakti
freyja

athena
mary
isis
aphrodite

sophia
saraswati
nut
faronika

inanna
kannon
gaia
venus

lemanja
mami wata
fatima
persephone

light
energy
emergence
womanhood

birthgiving
nourishing
essential
carrier of life

now is your time

approaching the fire

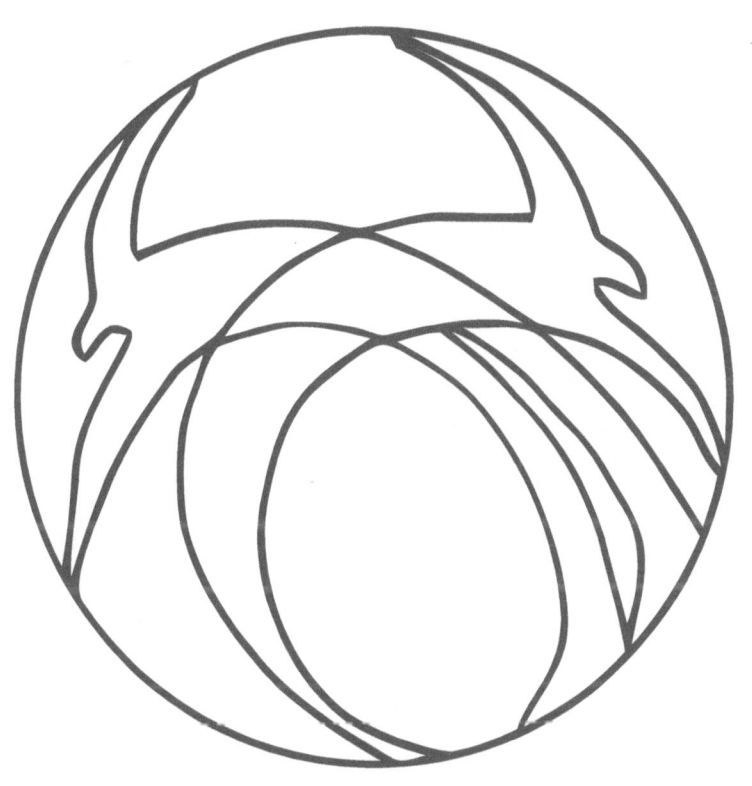

jumptime

dedicated to jean houston

did you ever
burst into life ?
not into laughter
or into tears
but into life ?

life calls you
to do just that
with all your senses
with all your non-sense
unfiltered, unpolished
off the record

expose your tender rawness
unleash your lavish appetite for love
exude your matchless fragrance

where were you all these years ?
asks life

jump off the cliff of your illusions
fly !

the only risk you take
is to be ravaged by life's fire

but ... isn't that
what you are looking for ?

it's jumptime
giantheart
it's jumptime

jump !

through my eyes

you have
not seen
the world
as only l
can see it

but if
you looked
at it
right through
my eyes
the universe
would all
be one
with you

oh step aside
my friend
and let
my eyes
be yours

what does
the burning
ot your
small world
matter ?

if you
at last
could see
the one
true life
you've always carried
in your soul

beyond

beyond
expression
is the subtlety
of now

gone
are the days
of surface chatter

behold
the rawness
of the spark
rekindled

it is
the only
honest guide
to life

rare

rare
are the roads
to heaven

why ?

not many dare
to build their
path to paradise

with only love
as pavement

with but a soulsong
as their guide

gold

dedicated to ibrahim abouleish

gold
is the colour
of our deepest tears

mined
in the mountains
of eternity

each drop
contains the essence
of a thousand oceans

one drop
could heal us all

forever

mount kailash

for thousand years
l have been waiting
on my mountain

for you to see me
and to start ascending

what is contained in you
looks for a home
a new one
so much larger
than the old

the time has come
for you to build your vessel

as you begin to rise
see me in every step

l am the threefold
trident trismegistus
the third force
you were looking for

you cannot walk alone
you need the other
and even more
you need the third

that force
that helps you grow
and climb without return

leave everything behind
but her

kailash is waiting
l'll be there

hesitation

l have traversed
my continent
a thousand times
to find the ocean

now at its shore
l hesitate to sail

though l well know
its waves are carriers
to eden

flow

let life just flow
without obstruction
through your veins

watch how you flourish friend
watch how it cures your pains

go deeper then
and flow with life
to its own source

and know your self
completely
know your purpose
essence, force

zero

becoming essential
is the call of our time

moving from experience to essence
breaking through illusion
being stark naked
crystal-clear

now

responding to each moment
as it arises
to rise with it
within it

that's it

not being separate
but part of it
integral part
becoming whole

one

one I
one you
one we
just one

zero

rainmaker

a drop of light
fell into me
from nowhere

now here
I am

I never had
a more refreshing shower

since then
I'm thirsty

since then
I'm on my way
towards the rainmaker

II. initiation

at last

one recent night
l found myself
initiated
in the book
of life

as l began
to read
turning its pages
in my soul
l knew
you held
my hands
and led my
searching eyes

since then
l find
new pages
of this book
in every corner
of my life

since then
l know
at last
l'm walking
on my path

III. involution

stepping into the fire

for real

this time for real

no turning back

turn
inwards
upwards
downwards
forward

do not turn back !

you have received
a thousand invitations
for a thousand liberations

you played and skirted
dabbled, flirted
never really went for it

this time for real

step up
break open every door and window
of your absurdly fragile prison cell

step out
get naked
breathe the air of freedom

then whirl whirl whirl
your self
into the center of life's fire

don't leave a single trace behind

this time for real

the drums grow louder

the drums
grow louder
as he steps
into the womb
of the tribe

into the sacred circle
of the otherworld
facing the final fires
of his old existence

ready, almost
to surrender
to being, becoming
sacrifice

ready, now
to die
ready, finally
to live

set my tree on fire

how much more open
must I hold my heart
until you enter ?

like an overripe fruit
my heart is hanging
from the tree of my life

pluck it
inflame it
and set my tree on fire

my greatest longing
is to fuse
my flames
with yours

like autumn leaves

allow your words
to leave your lips
as autumn leaves
detach from trees

with ease

fully surrendered
to life's flow
they know
their time has come

to go

one word

and if you had
but one word
that you could take
from this world

one that holds everything
said and unsaid

one that carries you
to your self, without deviation

one that nourishes you
in eternity
and lets you grow
into infinity

yes ?

you know one ?

then carve it quickly
into the trunk
of your tree

and never again
turn away
your gaze

these quiet moments

it is these quiet moments
that I cherish most

I see myself afresh
like from a vantage post

it's as if life undresses
revealing what seemed lost

it is these quiet moments
that I cherish most

deep down

stillness
alone
is the path
to the emergence
of your answers
from the lake
of existence
hidden
deep
down
in
your
and
my
one
self

prayer

oh make my deepest knowing
accessible to me
oh make my inner zone
a spirit library

awake my highest being
set me free
and take me in your dome
for all eternity

III. involution

oh let the world...

oh let the world
flow through my veins
let me be wide awake
for you who reigns
sustains the cosmic soul

make me your humble bowl
use, fill, refill and empty me
until l taste eternity
until l am – like you – pure cosmic breath
transcending life, transcending death

book of life

and what if
we read
every day
one page
of the book
of life

carefully

word by word
breath by breath
thought by thought
feeling by feeling
movement by movement
smile by smile
tear by tear
fear by fear

...

there is still
so much
to uncover

each page
holds the whole

let's sit by candlelight
and read, together

carefully

word by word
breath by breath

....

anew

anew anew
make every moment fresh
allow surprise to be your guide
throw open all your doors and windows

let every visitor
become your teacher
invite each one to add
a new log to your furnace

burn, daily, with each piece to ashes
trust being fed, anew, tomorrow

living temple

don't join the people
on their pilgrimage
to temples and cathedrals
made of walls
each but a host
to one of many faiths

become a living temple
made of light
with arms so wide
that you embrace
the world
as one

returning home

that which you seek,
my brother, in this world
is seeking you
in your own home

return
sit in your living room
and make a fire

after the night
the sun will rise
and for the first time ever
you'll be there

why now ?

infinite yearning
for finally returning

home

to what l've always known !

why did you make
me wait
so long ?

why is it now
you fill my cup
when l was almost
giving up ?

lll. involution

breakpoint

my little bucket
is about to break

you poured yourself
so totally
into my heart
that l can't hold
my self together
any longer

allow my cup
to burst into your stream
and as l join your waters
take me to your source

a single, longing heart

a valley
filled with fog
has no perception
of its depth
nor of the sun above it

engulfed in grey
it lies forgotten
motionless, confused

until a child
cries out for love
so wildly
that the clouds
are torn apart
by sun rays
eager to be seen and felt
in all their glory

god never chose
to be alone
in heaven

a single, longing heart
can call him home

grow, grow, grow

what then in you, my friend
than your heart
could have the strength
and spaciousness
to become
an abode
for the one

don't wait a moment, friend
but grow, grow, grow
your heart into a shrine
larger than any temple ever built

and as you build it
notice, how the one
is working in you
through you, with you

oh, how he is longing for a home !

see, it's like lovers
separated by a river
building a bridge from both sides

none of them can await
the glorious day
of completion

gateway

the great one
searches for the key
to your existence

can you not see
what you could be
if you surrendered ?

empty your house
and open wide
all doors and windows

and breathe
from now on
everlasting joy

there is
no other reason
for your life

your earthly presence:
but a gateway
to eternity

past to future

l lived
my friend
through endless variations
exaggerations
deviations
and inflations

from now on
friend
l turn my energy
with full intensity
to clarity
divinity
infinity

if you
my friend
walked by my side
we'd travel twice as fast
from past
to future

knocking on your door

why is it
that whenever
l knock on your door
your entire house
vibrates, throbs and thunders
like a reverberating temple bell
transporting me
to utter ectasy ?

then you open
for a short breath only
twinkling at me
with this simple, innocent smile
as if nothing had happened

beloved
why do you torture me ?
do you not see
how much l suffer ?

here l stand
reduced to nothing
but love
for you

living only
for the day
you invite me
into your home

a thousand years

a thousand years
of wandering
the earth

has brought me
to your doorstep
master

for thousand years
I've come
to learn your craft

for many thousands more
I vow to share
the harvest of your seeding

will you
accept me
in your cloister ?

say yes !
let fiery spring
transform my winter heart !

hold court

hold court, beloved
in my dying world

use my remaining breaths
as bricks to build your castle

oh let there be a single giant ballroom
in which my reborn self
can whirl forever
in your name

threshold

searching
for a place
beyond words
beyond time
I arrived
at your doorstep

there was
no name
on the gate
no bell
to ring

but you opened
the moment
I knelt
at your threshold

there was
no room
reserved
for me

love
has no address

and light
always moves

the weaver's song

your life
is but a carpet
of experiences
loosely tied together

you call this fabric "I"

how little do you know

look for the one
who makes the knots
wake up and join
the weaver's song

the more...

the more
I look
into the mirror
of my soul

the less
I find
the man
I thought
I am

the more
I look
into the mirror
of my soul

the more
I find
the light
I thought
I'm not

the more
I look
into the mirror
of my soul

the more
I am

reminder

last night
while I was fiercely praying
you knocked abruptly on my door

disguised
as my vexatious neighbour

my soul
had warned me
just in time

I asked you in
made tea
and lit a fire

I even offered
food and wine

I caught you winking at my soul

thank you !

now I can see you everywhere

in everything
in everyone
I find
the answer
to my prayer

new beginning

what poem
would I write
if all my words
were burned ?

what new expressions
would I birth
from ashes ?

with hands
led by the winds alone ?

oh firebird: emerge
and guide me home !

IV. elevation

rising from the ashes

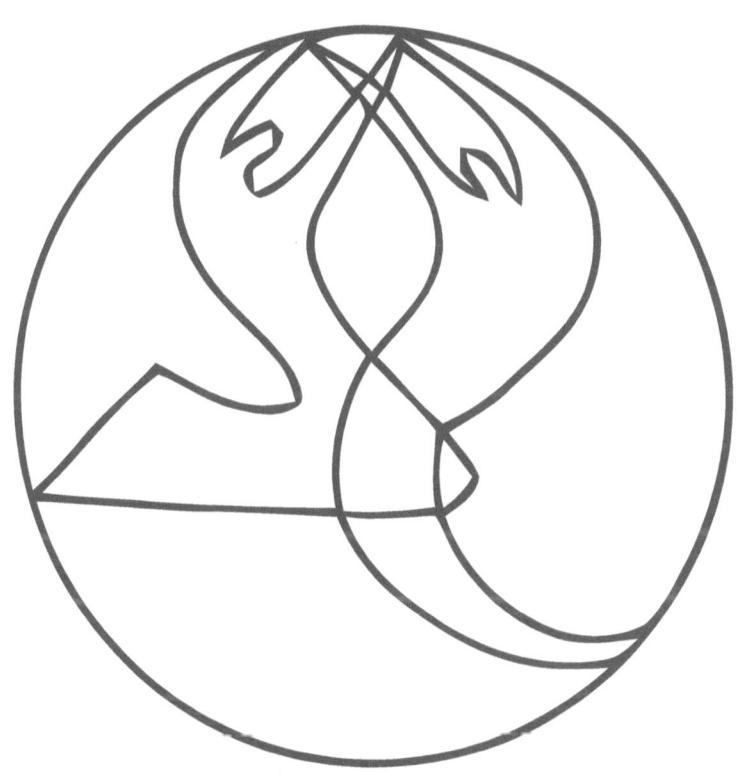

take off

who bothers
being called
a madman
when eternity
is calling ?

life
is an invitation
for liberation

hesitation
is for the dead

turn thoughts
to wings

take off !

love is looking for a dance partner

wild one
wake up

love is looking
for a dance partner

did you not know
that prayer has many forms ?

love is a passionate river
longing to flood your heart

yearning to dance you
to the ocean

wax and wick

one day
the candle
woke up
to the fact
that her
true nature
was not
wax and wick

but that all
that really "mattered"
was the flame
she nurtured

that day
her flame
became part
of the one
great fire

lionlike

live life
lionlike

potent
peacefulness

earthshaking
eros

side by side

becoming the earth drum

quietly
moulding
soulsands

surfacing
timeless
patterns

evoking
heartbeat
alignment

becoming
the earthdrum

playing her song

what a joy !

sound

once you dwell
at the birthplace
of sound

your thirst
for words
will be stilled

and your speech
shall flow
like honey
from heaven

prepared for miracles

don't call me poet
call me gatherer

I just collect
the pearls of life
arriving at my shores
from unseen depths
of timeless oceans

you always find me waiting
patiently, for silent treasures

with open palms
prepared for miracles

birth

since l was born
my heart is pregnant
with heaven

time to give birth
is it not ?

and time to bid farewell

because l know
that my shell
will break
into a thousand pieces

and as the god bursts forth
l shall be gone

skywards

soar skywards friend
towards the answer

your house
does not need
its ceiling
any longer

you have literally
grown too tall

and the skies
you now scrape
are rainless
and lit up with stars

stardust

stardust
crystallised

that's me
that's you
that's who we are

now we know
why we long
for the heavens

now we know
why we reach
for the stars

now we know
we can create
heaven on earth

you and l

my ship
was sailing
on your ocean

l liked
to think
my ship
is who
"l am"

until the day
you took
my vessel
in a storm

lost
was the ship
and every man

surviving
only
was
"l am"

well, yes
l lost
but more
l won

as now
your sea
and l
are one

we are ocean

new life is pulsing
in our worlds and words

as waves, unstoppable
we rise towards the heavens

from now on we are ocean
all-embracing bubbling ecstasy

that is the life
that has been waiting in us

all along

wildfire

I could
not find
the land
of endless possibilities
in the wide world

I found it
in my wild heart
that knows no boundaries
no foreigners
no police
no president

love
is the only dish
it serves

cooked
in the wildfire
of creation

cooked in paradise

tell me, my friend
about your new diet

you have grown
remarkably in size
since our last encounter

your heart is now so much wider
your words carry more weight
your laughter is round and fat
and your steps sink
so much deeper
into the earth

there you sit
like a chinese buddha
holding your butterball belly
with sparkling eyes
overflowing with appetite
for more

surely
your food
must have been cooked
in paradise

please

may I
reserve
a seat
at your table ?

every day

each cell of mine
is ripe to melt
into acceptance
of the fullness
of existence

embracing all
its wonders, perils
sweet encounters
sour tastes

too long
I have
been hiding
from the weather

from now on
I walk naked
through the seasons

fully exposed
immersed in oneness
rising, living, dying
every day

like an antenna

like an antenna
on a mountaintop
artfully tuned
to sense
the slightest whisper

fully erect
from birth to death
hardwired
to make love
with the divine

anchored in granite
kissing skies
a place to nest and rest
for birds and angels

unmoved by weathers
seasons, working hours
exposed to the essential
exploring the beyond
locating ever finer orbs

instantly
sharing its findings
with every listening soul

...

that's what I'd say
if you would ask me
what's a life worth living

wisdom

pour all your gifts
into the golden vessel
of this moment

it's not for you
to tame abundance
mother of all life

flow
is the flavour
of eternity

and love
is the face
of isis

I noticed
you are now
growing fruit trees
in her orchard

I never met
a wiser man

white

white poem
on white paper

beloved

is what I offer
at your altar

my fiery, boundless love
for you
did not allow
for words and verses

mute I stand before you
spacious like a white scroll
awaiting its scribe

a humble mirror
of your all-embracing snow-white sun

god

the god
that occupies
my sky
my earth
and every cell
of every life
is everywhere
as if
he she it
wanted
needed
to be found
by you, by me
by everyone
to fully be
forever
one

passion

you may hear passion
in my voice
at times

perhaps you feel
as if I'm acting
in a theatre

well, well ...

... it does explain
that I see life
as one great stage
on which I play
with all my guts

no holding back
but humbled
by the fact
that life's great playwright
is the master
that I serve

each morning

my ear
each morning
reaches out

to meet
the early greetings
of my garden birds

to host
the finest murmur
of my soul

each morning
is a new beginning

each chirp
each whisper
is a blessing

how rich these days
of silent presence
wordless stillness

when garden
birds and soul
are all but unborn notes
in life's one song

pearl song

the day
she took
her question
to the temple

surrendered
and entrusted it
to higher spheres

a song
of utmost beauty
filled her heart

wrapped
carefully
in solemn strophes

she found
the pearl
she had been praying for

music

being the bow
in the tender hands
of the universal musician

playing the one timeless symphony
composed of the myriads of notes
that we all together are ...

... what more could we possibly ask for ?

let's place our selves gently
on his lush meadows

like priceless wedding gifts
and trust that he shall pick us up

no need to wait long

his longing
is as great
as ours

god's sitar
dedicated to paul grant

imagine your self
as god's sitar

placed on his lap
serving his genius

every now and then
you would need to be finetuned

each time you return to stage
newer and finer sounds stream out of you

with every year of service
you express more, with less notes

till the day comes
when his touch
and your tone
are one

overflowing

my heart is like a beehive
filled with honey
from a thousand trees
collected by a thousand bees

I do confess, my heart is overflowing
with sweetest love, and growing growing
is the queen inhabiting its core
preparing to invite the world, and more

not my hand
but my heart
holds the pen
through which flows
the one word
big enough
to contain
the essence
of my love
for you ...

your name

...over
and
over
again

my favourite country

your heart
is my favourite country

a country
without people
and yet: so full of life

a country
without borders
and yet: it contains me completely

a country
without trees
and yet: so full of miraculous blossoms

a country
without government
and yet: governed by beauty and balance

a country
I never shall leave
as long as it beats for me

your heart
is my favourite country

mountaintop

no, l do not feel remote from life
now that my hut is on a mountaintop

by holding dear the highest in my heart
l simply grew and with me rose the earth

my little hut has never changed
nor has its distance from the ground

but constant travel added many layers
and brought me closer to the sun

up here, l'm so much nearer to life's mystery
keep walking, friend, you'll soon be joining me

single taste

we have not danced together yet
within your soul's great banquet hall
but I do long to meet you there
one moonlit, passionate night
to waltz and whirl with you
into the single taste
of all beginnings
and all ends

the poem you are

the poem
that you are

is inscribed
since time immemorial

in the bark
of the tree
that l am

one

one word
one gaze
one touch
one gesture

how can
you fill
so much
in "one" ?

you say
that "one"
is all
there is

you I
we they
are all
but "one"

one light
one breath
one life
one death

sacred union

don't ever turn
your laser gaze
away from me

this is the essence
of the sacred union
you are longing for

stay tuned, attuned
become the song of life

and whirl and turn
as I myself would do

bury your name
become pure flame

and as you rise to heaven
join my skies
as evershining star

afterlude

firebird's secret

I am

my heart
is throbbing
with love

I drop
this little cup
I am
no more

the cosmos
is now
my chalice

I
hold
it
holds
me

does it matter ?

I am !

post-mortem poem

who will remember

these thruths ?

who will remember these truths ?

where does the sun rise
if not in my inner eye ?

where do the stars dance
if not in my mind's sky ?

where dwells the moon at midday
if not in my cradling heart ?

and who receives postcards from god
if not my amorous soul ?

it's all so obvious
is it not ?
and yet
they call me a madman

but then
who will remember these truths
when I have left this world
together with the sunrise
the stars and the moon
leaving no address behind ?

index of poems

IV. elevation: rising from the ashes

afterlude: firebird's secret

post-mortem poem

artists' biographies

alexander schieffer
poetry

alexander schieffer pursues an integral path to life in ser- vice of the holistic deve- lopment of hu- manity. he is, simultaneously, a transformative educator, engaged activist, passio- nate community builder, integral philosopher, and spiritual poet. he lives, together with his wife and poet-performer-acti- vist rama mani in the french countryside near geneva, where both are co-creating a "home for humanity". this place also serves as seat and rural campus for trans4m, a center for in- tegral development that alexander co-founded, and which has evolved into a "local global movement for the integral renewal of people and planet" – active in africa, middle east, europe, asia and south america. his books in english include integral development, integral economics, transformation manage- ment, and integral research and innovation – as well as a ger- man poetry volume entitled niemandsland.

www.trans-4-m.com

marko pogačnik
cosmograms

born in 1944, marko pogačnik lives in šempas, slovenia. during the years 1965-71, he worked in conceptual art and land art as a member of the oho group. exhibitions followed in aktionsraum, munich, museum of modern art, new york, and the biennale at venice. after 1971, he worked in the field of art combined with integral ecology (geomancy). he has developed a method of earth healing called "lithopuncture", complemented with the "language of cosmograms". lithopuncture works are standing in many countries of europe plus kazakhstan, south africa, brazil, ecuador, canada and usa. since 1998, he develops "gaia touch" body exercises to tune to the essence of the earth. his books in english include: touching the breath of gaia, turned upside down, nature spirits & elemental beings, gaia's quantum leap, sacred geography. in 2015, he was appointed a unesco artist for peace by the secretary general of unesco.

www.markopogacnik.com